D0527184

Garden
Succulents

RHS WISLEY HANDBOOKS

Garden
Succulents

Terry Hewitt

THE ROYAL HORTICULTURAL SOCIETY

The right of Terry Hewitt to be identified as the author
of this work has been asserted by him in accordance with
the Copyright, Designs and Patents Act 1988.

First published in Great Britain in 2003 by
Cassell Illustrated
Octopus Publishing Group
2–4 Heron Quays, London E14 4PJ

A CIP catalogue record for this book is available
from the British Library
ISBN 1 84403 077 6

Commissioning Editor: Camilla Stoddart
Editor: Robin Douglas-Withers
Designer: Justin Hunt

Printed in China

Contents

Previous page:
Beschorneria
yuccoides

INTRODUCTION

From the frozen Arctic tundra to the hot, dry deserts and the hot, humid tropics, plants grow all over the world. Each habitat has its own unique flora that has adapted to survive in these very different conditions. This explains why plants that grow rapidly in warm, high-rainfall areas will often languish under drier or cooler conditions; the converse is also true, slow-growing plants that have adapted to conserve moisture in more arid areas are often swamped by faster-growing plants and grasses when put into more lush surroundings.

WHAT ARE SUCCULENT PLANTS?

Around the world are many desert areas where rainfall is occasional and unreliable. During the dry season these appear barren but they are quite different after the rains. Lying dormant in the soil are the seeds of many annuals and these can germinate, grow, flower and set seed all in the very short space of time when rain falls. This is one method of overcoming erratic rainfall. Another is for the plants to adapt their form and growing cycle to store water when it is available and then use it slowly until the next rainfall. While some plants capable of this are woody (*xerophytes*), the majority are succulent. Succulents have evolved methods of storing moisture in their leaves, stems or roots and these enable them to survive long periods of drought.

Plants lose most of their moisture through their leaves or flowers, but in most succulents the leaves are thick and usually have far fewer stomata (breathing pores) and a thickened waxy

Hesperaloe parviflora looks striking here when planted amongst other perennials.

6

coating. Many succulents have a globular or hemispherical shape as this is the best way to have the maximum volume of tissue with the minimum surface area. In addition, to prevent their skin splitting as they swell when taking up water, or wrinkling when they are dry, many of these plants are ribbed like an accordion. The ribbing also creates a microclimate and the ribs cast shadows on neighbouring parts of the plant. Many succulent plants flower during or just before the wet season and form their seedpods; these may take months to ripen but are scattered or distributed in time for the next wet period.

Succulent plants occur in many different plant families and have developed many weird and wonderful forms. The tall, branched saguaro (*Carnegiea gigantea*), often seen in cowboy western films, and the flat, dinner plate-like segmented branches of the prickly pear (*Opuntia ficus-indica*) are familiar to most of us. The wonderful thick swollen trunk of the enormous African baobab tree (*Adansonia* spp) is another of nature's curiosities. Other examples of the diversity of these plants are the money, or jade, plant (*Crassula ovata*) with its thick fleshy leaves, the aloes with their healing properties, and the stone plants (*Lithops* spp) with their tiny swollen leaves.

Probably the best workable definition of succulents I have seen is 'those plants normally cultivated by succulent plant collectors' (man's desire to collect the unusual, the bizarre and the weird has made many succulent plants very popular). Trying to define a succulent botanically, however, is extremely difficult. For example, some, but not all, bulbous plants are considered succulent, as are some members of the cucumber family, but not cucumbers themselves. While the majority of modified plants tend to come from the hottest and most arid places in the world, not all succulents grow in hot habitats: there are a number of exceptions, such as stonecrops (*Sedum*) and navelwort (*Umbilicus*) and alpine houseleeks (*Sempervivum*). These mostly low-growing succulents are often described as alpines or rockery plants in British garden centres, as they need little winter protection in British gardens.

NATURAL HABITATS

The cactus family is a large one and only contains succulents. Cacti are native to the Americas, growing from just into Canada through to Chile and Argentina. The few species that come from cold areas are often protected by a covering of snow in winter or survive because the winters are dry with a very low humidity. These are often difficult keep alive through the dark, cold and wet winters that are more usual in Britain.

Africa covers much the same latitudes as the Americas but has given rise to a much more diverse flora. There are no cacti, but there are many different plant families that have adapted to the more arid areas (such as the euphorbias), often giving rise to plants with a broadly similar shape to the cacti of the Americas because they've independently evolved to survive in similar habitats.

A typical habitat for many of these plants is desert, a habitat characterised by its scarce rainfall (experiencing less than 25cm (10in) of rain per annum), where succulent plants are usually found growing on poor and very free-draining soils. Rainfall is highly variable in these habitats, usually with a marked or prolonged dry season, and some years bring no rain at all. In the harshest areas plants are usually small, and during the dry season some succulents may literally pull themselves down into the soil by their roots. Germination often takes place in the shade of rocks or other small shrubs or bushes. Some succulents grow in arid grassland where the dried grasses give some protection from the hottest sun, but these plants would be suffocated by lusher vegetation.

Deserts are also well-known for their soaring temperatures, but these can plummet at night, especially in cold deserts (those at high altitudes), where freezing temperatures are not unusual in winter. Coastal deserts, such as the Atacama and the Namib are strongly influenced by mists that roll in off the sea, which increase humidity and moderate temperatures; plants in these regions have evolved mechanisms to collect this airborne moisture.

Cultivation, pests and diseases

Among the succulents are some beautiful plants and, although specialist growers may prefer to keep them in heated glasshouses, many make fine specimens for use outdoors during the frost-free months of the year. Many are easy to grow, adding extra interest to a garden, patio or balcony with their interesting shapes, colours and textures. And, so long as the gardener is prepared for failures in severe winters, a great deal of pleasure can be had from experimenting with more unusual varieties to find what is hardy in a particular area.

I garden in Sussex, 11 miles from the coast, and I have found that few succulents will survive outdoors here during the winter, although friends and contacts in milder parts of the country have found several species that they can keep permanently outdoors. A much wider range can be enjoyed, even in cooler climates, if the plants are grown in pots in the garden during summer and brought into a greenhouse where they are protected from frost during the winter.

Growing plants in gardens means to some extent trying to emulate what they experience in their natural habitat and in the case of succulents this is generally free-draining soil, occasional rainfall, low humidity and usually no frosts. While it may be possible to mimic some requirements, others, such as light and humidity, are not readily reproduced. Therefore there has to be compromise.

The easiest part to achieve is a well-drained growing medium. The amount of water the plants receive can be adjusted by protecting them from the natural elements if, for

Echeveria glauca with red and yellow flowers growing amongst rocks.

example, there is a long period of summer rain. The low humidity (around 10–15 per cent) experienced by some of these plants in their natural habitat is seldom achieved in Britain, while, in the relatively low light levels of the northern latitudes, full sun in summer is perhaps the equivalent of medium shade in more equatorial latitudes.

The need for frost protection means that currently in most parts of the British Isles, the plants will need to be brought indoors for the winter. (If our winters are reverting back to the warmer type experienced in the earlier part of the last millennium, then there will be an increasing number of species that may grow permanently outdoors.) For those areas that are virtually frost free or rarely experience temperatures lower than about -5°C (23°F) – usually coastal or in the larger urban conurbations, such as London – there are a limited number of succulent plants that seem able to survive outside, However, cool, wet winters seem to be as destructive as very low temperatures, and even plants that have been established outdoors for some while are likely to succumb during unusual periods of sub-zero temperatures or high rainfall.

OUTDOOR BEDS

If you are fortunate enough to live in a virtually frost-free area, it is certainly worth trying a small bed of the more robust succulents. This is unlikely to prove much more expensive than one of bedding plants – which nobody expects to survive the

Aloe arborescens produces brilliant red flowers in winter.

winter – and will certainly be different. By experimenting over several years you will find those plants that do best under your conditions; as the weather in Britain is very localized,these may be quite different to those only a mile away. Larger plants are usually more robust than small ones, but, at best, most succulents are only borderline hardy. If severe weather is forecast, protect the bed with fleece or something similar to minimize the risk of damage.

A sunny, south-facing slope, well protected from the wind, is the ideal site. Dig the ground well and add about 50 per cent gravel into the top 15cm (6in).The slope will enable any surplus water to drain freely away. If there is no convenient slope, raise the bed above the normal soil level to assist with drainage.

During summer, unless there are prolonged periods of drought, most of these plants will only require the occasional watering. Many will tell you when they are short of water by hanging their leaves or appearing shrivelled. Beds will always hold a lot more water than pots.

POTS

In pots the growing medium is extremely important.The plants must have a well-drained compost, which can usually be achieved by adding small grit (crushed if possible), 1:3 by volume, to a proprietary compost, either loam-based or soilless. Alternatively, mix equal amounts by volume of loam-based compost, soilless compost and grit.The loam is heavier and will help to stabilize the mix, while the soil-less compost will add fibre for porosity.The gravel will add extra weight to the pot for stability and help prevent it from becoming waterlogged.

Where the plants are to be displayed outdoors, use unglazed terracotta containers as this will improve drainage during periods of heavy rain. The additional weight will also help to keep the pots stable in windy situations.

Choosing a pot

Plants should look 'comfortable' in their containers. Before potting the plant, stand it in the container and see how it looks. If it does not look right, find a different pot. Choose one that the plant easily fits into, with perhaps a couple of centimetres of space all around, so that there is room for growth. Low growing or globular plants look best in shallow containers about 9–13cm (3½–5in) deep. Tall, bushy or tree-like specimens need full-depth pots, both for stability and room to grow. The size depends on the height and bulk of the plant. If the container is too small the plant will not have room to grow and will topple in the lightest breeze. Some spreading plants also look their best when placed in a taller pot or urn-shaped container, which allows plenty of room for the stems to trail down the sides.

The choice of container also depends on the site. In general, natural and subdued colours help to display plants at their best. If pots are to be plunged into a bed, then clay or terracotta are best as they will allow some moisture to percolate through the sides of the pot as well as through the bottom. If they are for individual display on a patio or for a focal point, then a more elaborate container may enhance the attractions of the plant. Stone sinks or troughs make good natural settings for multiple plantings. Broad, shallow plastic containers can also be used and are a great deal lighter to move around the garden – make sure they have adequate drainage holes. Avoid containers without drainage holes as these easily become waterlogged in wet weather or due to over-zealous attention from the gardener.

Potting

Having found the right container, place a piece of mesh over the drainage hole to stop insects and slugs from nesting in the bottom. Cover the base of the pot with a layer of gravel to assist with drainage. Most plants (except the very tall ones) only need a compost depth of about 15cm (6in) at most. With taller pots include a deeper layer of gravel, leaving sufficient room at the top for planting. Use a light material, such as broken polystyrene, to fill the surplus space in deep, wide containers, preventing the compost from drifting down into it with a few sheets of newspaper. This keeps the container much lighter and so easier to move.

Remove the plant from its pot and break up the rootball, shaking out as much of the old compost as possible. Failure to do this often means that water will not penetrate through the interface of the old and new compost, leaving one wet and one

Haworthia
attenuata
*'Biettemana' grows
well in pots.*

dry. Position the plant in the new container at the same height
that it was in old one, leaving enough space at the top of the
pot for watering, then fill with compost, firming as you go. Pots
can be top dressed with a small gravel, which will help to
support the plant, keep the surface of the soil fresh and conserve
moisture in long dry spells. A natural type of stone dressing also
enhances the display.

If you are making a multiple planting, leave space between
the plants to allow them to grow; planted too close, the
strongest will probably swamp the others. When the container
is fully planted, arrange some pieces of rock between the plants
before adding any top dressing. You should now have a small,
natural-looking landscape.

Smaller plants will probably outgrow their containers in a
year or two and should then be repotted. An ideal time to do
this is in the spring, when new growth has just started. They
will then rapidly settle down into their new surroundings. Most
other plants, except for the very large ones, will probably
benefit from repotting every two to three years. Old compost
can become very compacted and restrict the percolation of
water and air to the roots.

Watering

Most of the plants in this book are summer-growing. There are others with different growing seasons but many of these like to be dry during their dormant period – unlikely in a British summer!

Plants will only grow when the moisture content of the compost is between an upper and lower limit. If it is too wet, the plant cannot breathe and longish periods of waterlogged soil will soon rot the roots. If it is kept dust dry for long periods, then the root hairs will die and have to re-grow when water is next available. The ideal, therefore, is to wait until the compost is just dry and then to water. With large containers, give sufficient water at a time, so that the compost will dry out in about 10 days. Small containers will dry out much more quickly and require more frequent watering. The best guide is given by a moisture meter, available from most garden centres and DIY stores. They cost little more than a plant does and will pay their way in a relatively short space of time. Most people will find that they only need to water about half as often as they think – wait until the meter reads at the low end of the scale before watering again.

Unless you live in an area with a very high chalk content, tap water is quite suitable for watering. Rainwater can be used if it is available.

During the winter months most cacti and succulent plants do not require any watering. Keep them almost dry from October through to March and during low temperatures of 5°C (41°F) or less. If they are brought indoors into a warm environment of 15–20°C (59–68°F), they should be kept almost dry during December and January. Water should only be given if they are showing signs of excessive dehydration, and then only in small amounts. The short days and low light levels during winter mean that growth will be weak and often etiolated and more susceptible to infection than growth hardened in the autumn.

Feeding

Like all living things, if you put nothing in, you get little out! Although these plants come from arid areas, the upper soil crust is often rich in mineral deposits left by evaporating moisture. These become available to the plant during the rains or are dissolved by the often heavy night dews and mists.

In cultivation, succulents will rapidly respond to a well-balanced cactus food (or one suitable for tomatoes, fed at half strength). Growth will be stronger, healthier and more floriferous than in those that survive on just water. For best results, feed the plants every one to two weeks from March until September.

Light

In Britain the light levels even in summer are low in comparison with the tropics. Here most succulents are best in full sun, whereas in Arizona, for example, the longer hotter days often mean that the same plants need some shade. Most of the plants will thrive in a bright situation, even if full sun can not be provided.

If your plants are overwintered indoors, put them out into the shade initially to acclimatize. Dull, overcast days are ideal, enabling them to become accustomed to the extra light more slowly. After one to two weeks in the shade, move them to their final positions.

Temperature

Most of these plants prefer a minimum temperature above 6°C (43°F) and will tolerate much higher temperatures than other plants in the garden. If it gets too hot, they tend to go to sleep for a while and wake up again when the temperature lowers. Whilst dormant, the plants will stop growing, and leafy species will shed some of their leaves.

Although some come from areas with low winter temperatures, many are either insulated from the cold by a covering of snow or are extremely dehydrated at the onset of winter due to low rainfall; in some cases the only water these plants receive each year is from the melting snow. In cultivation in the British Isles, these plants suffer at low temperatures because of the high humidity and lack of light. This means that many of the naturally hardy species can be quite troublesome to keep through the winter, even in a greenhouse. There are just a few species that may survive outdoors in planted beds and a small number that will survive if they are protected from rain so that they are completely dry in winter. A temperature of about 11°C (50°F) in winter will allow a very wide range of plants to be grown.

Puya alpestris.

Keeping plants healthy

Succulents are wonderful plants for the busy person as they survive with the minimum of care. They are used to tolerating unpredictable weather patterns in the wild so periods of neglect are no problem to them. However, for the best results, plants in pots should be watered when dry, fed with a fertilizer every couple of weeks (see above) and protected from low temperatures (see above). If this is done most should grow quite happily, although slowly.

Pests and diseases

Succulents suffer from the usual range of plant pests, but pesticides sometimes damage them so their use should be limited to situations where they are really needed. The risk of damage can be reduced by not treating plants that are in bright sunshine, or exposed to extremes of temperature, or are in a dehydrated condition. Biological controls are entirely safe and will give effective control of some pests when conditions are suitable. They can be ordered through some garden centres or by mail order from specialist firms, which will also advise on the conditions required by a particular control.

Vine weevil

Most succulents are susceptible to vine weevil but especially *Sedum*, *Crassula* and *Echeveria*. The larvae are plump, creamy white, legless grubs with slightly curved bodies, up to 10mm (½in) long, and pale brown heads. They eat plant roots and can bore up into the stems of succulents. Infested plants collapse and die, although it is sometimes possible to rescue them by taking cuttings from above the point of damage. Pot plants can be protected by treating the compost with a drench of imidacloprid in mid- to late summer, while the plants are in active growth. Biological control is available in the form of a pathogenic nematode, *Steinernema kraussei*, which infects the grubs with a fatal bacterial disease. It is best applied in August and can be used on pot plants and in the open soil. However, it can be effective at soil temperatures down to 5°C (41°F), so can be applied later if necessary.

Red spider mite

During the summer, tiny mites, up to 1mm long, may infest the stems and foliage of many plants. Despite their name, they are

Opuntia humifusa, growing here amongst gravel and rocks.

yellowish green with darker markings. Damaged leaves and stems develop a fine pale speckling or silvery brown discoloration. In heavy attacks a fine silk webbing appears on the plant and the foliage may drop prematurely. Pesticide resistance is common with red spider mite and so biological control with a predatory mite, *Phytoseiulus persimilis*, is often the best option.

Aphids – greenfly and blackfly

These are an occasional problem with succulents. They infest the growing points and the flowers. The presence of cast white skins on the foliage is often the first indication of their presence. Aphids excrete a sticky substance, called honeydew, which can be colonized by a black sooty mould. Treat infested plants with imidacloprid, either as a compost drench on pot plants, or use a spray formulation on the foliage. Other insecticides that will control aphids are bifenthrin, pyrethrum and rotenone (derris).

Mealybugs

These will not be a problem on hardy succulents but they may build up on plants that are kept indoors for winter. These greyish-white sap-feeding insects cluster in the leaf axils. They cover themselves with a fluffy white waxy substance that gives them a certain amount of protection from water-based sprays and they can be difficult to control. Sprays based on fatty acids or plant oils, such as rape seed oil, help to dissolve the wax. These sprays have little persistence and so need to be applied thoroughly on two or three occasions at one-week intervals.

Fungal and bacterial disease

These are not usually a problem in summer but can be in winter. Although some of them can be treated with proprietary cures, it is more important to find out the cause and correct it.

Over-watering is perhaps the cause of more deaths in succulents than any other. Always wait until plants have dried out before watering again (see p.16). If a plant has started to rot from the base, remove it from its pot immediately and shake off the surplus soil. Examine the stem: if it is still green then there is a chance of saving it. Allow it to dry for 1–2 weeks and examine it again. If there is no further rot, pot it up again and keep it on the dry side for a while until it re-establishes. If the stem is brown and (probably) soft, carefully pare away the rotten tissue to see how far the rot has gone. If it has gone right through the stem, gradually work up from the base, cutting through the stem until sound, clean tissue is found, continue until no threads of red or brown can be seen. If the rot has gone right through the plant's vascular system, little can be done, however, if not, the sound part of the plant can be restarted as a cutting (see p.24).

When the top of the plant rots, there are two likely causes. Firstly, that it has been frosted, and secondly that the humidity is too high for the temperature. A good air circulation (like outdoors) or a fan (in an enclosed space) will perhaps enable a reduction of 2°C (3.5°F) in the lowest temperature the plants will tolerate. As it is not practical to adjust the humidity beyond normal care, the alternative is to raise the temperature.

Cold, dull and damp conditions are the least favourable for these plants.

Close up of Notocactus leninghaussii.

PROPAGATION

There are two main methods of propagating succulents: by seed and by cuttings.

SEED

Most of the plants listed can be raised from seed, which is usually available from the more specialist catalogues, particularly those of cactus and succulent suppliers.

Sow seeds on the surface of a small container of gritty, well-drained compott, and then cover them with a thin layer of fine grit. They require a temperature of 21–27°C (70–81°F), so either use a propagator or hope that nature will provide the heat in summer. Keep the compost damp until the seeds have germinated; this takes 3–4 weeks for many species, although some may take several months.

Treat the seedlings much like the larger plants, watering them and then allowing them to almost dry before watering again. As they are comparatively slow growing, the earlier in the year they can be sown, the larger they will be by the first winter. During the winter, keep them almost dry unless a higher temperature of around 15°C (59°F) can be maintained. Seedlings are best left in their original containers until they are large enough to handle easily, as their fine root system is easily damaged.

CUTTINGS

Being able to multiply your plant collection (or rescue a plant that is dying) is one of the joys of gardening. Many succulents

Sedum 'Herbstfreude' (syn. Autumn Joy) is an easy herbaceous sedum that is loved by butterflies.

will root readily from cuttings, with just a few precautions, the main one being that most succulent cuttings should be left to callous until they have made a firm dry surface. In most cases this means leaving the cutting in a bright, warm and dry place for a few days. Slender, shrubby cuttings may be dry enough in 24 hours but those of a larger diameter may take 2–3 weeks in summer, 2–3 months in winter. The ideal time for taking cuttings is spring to early summer when nature should provide the ideal rooting and growing conditions.

For shrubby or bushy species, short semi-ripe cuttings work best – generally 5–10cm (2–4in) lengths are the easiest to deal with. Those that are too long will be difficult to keep straight until they have rooted, and if they become badly bent they may have to be cut again and re-rooted. Larger plants with tall, rigid stems, such as a tall cactus, can provide much longer cuttings; lengths of up to 1.5m (5ft) will take quite readily but must be dried for longer and may take from 3 months to 2 years to root.

Set the cuttings into a container half full of a gritty, open and free-draining compost, topped with fine grit. Push the cuttings through the grit into the compost, firm gently and lightly water. Keep the compost just damp; if it is too wet the cuttings will rot, and if it is completely dry the plants will not be encouraged to make roots. Several cuttings can be placed in the same pot or tray. With large cuttings that are much slower to root, fill a third of the pot with compost and cover this with a thin layer of grit. Stand the cutting on the grit then add more grit around it. This will help the cutting to stand upright without the base being wet, and yet there will be enough moisture given off by the compost to encourage rooting.

Place the pots or trays of cuttings in a warm, bright and airy position. When new growth is apparent, the cutting probably have rooted. Leave it for a further couple of weeks and then tip the cutting out and examine the base. If it has rooted, it can be potted individually, if not, put it back into the original pot and allow a little longer for it to root.

The flowers of Echinocereus pentalophus.

AN A-Z OF GARDEN SUCCULENTS

This section features the more robust species of succulent plants, those that are most likely to be able to survive in Britain. However, as there are many thousands of succulents and about 2,000 cacti, there will also be others that are well worth trying. As a rough guide, avoid plants that come from equatorial climates, unless they are from high altitudes. These are far less likely to survive the rigors of a British summer. (See p.10–19 for details on care and providing the best growing conditions.)

AEONIUM

These rosette-forming plants are mostly from the Canary Islands. Many are almost stemless or make small bushes, but some grow to about 1m (3ft) tall. They will tolerate low temperatures for short periods, but if the stems become frozen the plants will collapse in a rotten mass. The flowerhead develops from an elongation of the growing point of the rosette. Most species are spring-flowering, producing clusters of small, mostly yellow to cream flowers; the whole rosette dies after flowering.

The taller species make excellent feature plants in pots and can be used as summer bedding.

A. arboreum

This species grows to about 1m (3ft) tall, branching to make many dense rosettes, to 15cm (6in) across, of narrow bright green leaves. The plants flower in early spring, producing pyramids of small, golden-yellow flowers.

Aeonium arboreum.

As it tends to grow throughout the year, it will require a little water in winter. Wait until the leaves just begin to wilt before watering lightly. During the spring and summer, water frequently to keep a good head of leaves. It is an easy species to propagate from cuttings, which will root easily and rapidly in spring and summer if allowed to dry for a couple of days and then potted and kept just damp.

'**Atropurpureum**' is excellent as summer bedding with its deep purple leaves during the bright summer months. These revert to a deep green in the shade and during the darker winter months (see photo p.17).

Aeonium haworthii.

A. haworthii

This short bushy species has rosettes of short, thick, bluish leaves often tinged with red. Older plants make a beautiful, dense, hemispherical mound, some heads producing a creamy inflorescence in the spring.

A. 'Zwartkop'

This hybrid is a slightly darker shade than *A. arboreum* 'Atropurpureum' and better at keeping its purple colour throughout the year. It is also good for summer bedding.

AGAVE

This large genus of over 400 species has been subject to several revisions in recent years. All species are natives of the southern USA, south to northern South America, and through the Caribbean. They produce stemless, or nearly stemless, rosettes of green, bluish or grey leaves. The small species are no more than 15cm (6in) across when mature, while the large species can be several metres in diameter. They flower when mature – between five and forty years old – the growing point turning into the flower stem and the rosette dying after flowering. Normally, the plants offset during their life, making clumps of different sized rosettes.

Some agave species have been important crops for at least the last 9,000 years, being grown for food, for their fibre (sisal) and to make the spirit tequila from the fermented pulp. Because of their use to man, agaves have been widely cultivated and are now widespread in warm inhabited areas, such as the Mediterranean.

A few species seem to be relatively hardy in Britain, providing they can be protected from the winter rains and are grown in a very well-drained compost. A sheet of plastic placed over the rosette to keep the rain out of the crown may well be sufficient protection, so long as there is good air circulation around the plant. Although tolerant of low temperatures, many species are prone to rotting if water collects in the crown or on the curved surfaces of the leaves. Badly damaged leaves can be trimmed in the spring with a very sharp knife. As a general guide those plants that are native of the warmer climates tend to be of a paler green in colour, those from the colder areas tend towards bluish or greyish leaves.

All species make very attractive feature plants when grown in pots. Larger plants require substantial pots.

Apart from those listed below, other species that appear to be relatively hardy include *A. filifera*, *A. gracilipes*, *A. havardiana*, *A. lechuguilla*, *A. neomexicana*, *A. palmeri*, *A. scabra* and *A. utahensis*.

A. americana

This large bluish-leaved species is a common sight in the Mediterranean where it is extensively used as a bedding plant. With protection from winter rain, it is fairly tolerant of low

temperatures. The long slender leaves can grow to over 2m (6ft) long and it suckers freely to make large clumps, so it requires plenty of space. When mature the flower stem can attain a height of nearly 10m (30ft). While it is spectacular in a bed where weather conditions permit, it is probably too large for a pot.

Left: Agave americana.

Right: Agave americana 'Variegata'.

'**Mediopicta**' has variegated leaves – a yellow or white stripe in the centre. '**Mediopicta Alba**' is probably more common and has bluish leaves with a white to cream central stripe. It is a much smaller than the species and much better suited to pot culture. In a large urn-type pot, it makes a very impressive feature plant. '**Variegata**' has green leaves with deep cream to yellow margins. There appears to be a number of different forms, some more compact than others. It is very popular for landscaping and is often used in amenity horticulture as a summer-bedding plant.

Unfortunately these variegated forms of *A. americana* are nowhere near as hardy as the species and will only survive outdoors in a very sheltered environment.

A. lophantha

This smaller species, up to about 1m (3ft) across, has many forms, most of which have a pronounced pale yellowish-green band down the centre of each leaf. The leaves are generally fairly slender and narrow with very sharp teeth along their margins. Given good drainage, it is moderately hardy.

A. parasana

An attractive species, to about 1m (3ft) in diameter, with broad grey-blue leaves armed with strong teeth. This, one of the more impressive species, makes an excellent compact feature plant, larger specimens having an almost hemispherical silhouette. It is comparatively hardy when protected from the winter rain and can be used in a large container or for outdoor planting.

A. parryi

Agave parryi with Echevaria glauca, Alternanthera and Sedum spathulifolium used as summer bedding.

This species and its varieties must be the most photogenic of all the agaves. Its comparatively broad and short blue-grey leaves are tipped with black spines making it very eye-catching. Reaching about 1m (3ft) in diameter, it is comparatively slow growing taking perhaps 30–40 years to reach flowering size. Unfortunately, it is scarce in cultivation and not often available.

A. salmiana

This large species can attain a diameter of over 4m (12ft). Its leaves are long, broad and thickened at the base, making it very heavy. The edges of the leaves are fiercely spined and rigid. It seems to be relatively hardy when bedded out and is probably one of the toughest of the agaves.

ALOE

This large genus of mainly rosette-forming succulents from Africa and Madagascar ranges from small plants of 5cm (2in) in diameter to large trees. They are quite tropical in their requirements and, in general, those from southern Africa are the most hardy, particularly those from some of the mountainous areas.

Their wide variety of leaf shapes and colour and their different sizes make aloes superb feature plants for containers or for summer bedding. However, most are unsuitable for permanent outdoor bedding in Britain and will rot rapidly if frozen.

Those plants that produce offsets can be propagated from cuttings during the warm months, but the solitary ones need to be grown from seed.

A. arborescens

This robust bushy species offsets quite freely when small and produces brilliant red flowers in winter. The long, toothed blue-green leaves form a rosette up to about 75cm (30in) across and often take on a suffused purple tone during summer. Mature plants make large clumps up to 2m (6ft) tall (see photo p.12).

An excellent feature specimen in pots, this species is popular as a garden plant in South Africa.

A. aristata

Probably the most tolerant of all the aloes, this species will often survive outdoors if given a little protection from the weather. The stemless rosettes are up to 13cm (5in) in diameter and offset freely to make clumps. They consist of short and broad, pointed dark green leaves covered with whiskery, hair-like teeth that give the impression of cobwebs on the plant. During spring the leaves swell and orangey-red flowers are produced in early summer. On warmer and drier summer days, the leaves lose some of their turgidity and the rosette closes to a ball shape, the leaves incurved towards their tips.

An extremely easy and robust plant tolerating complete neglect.

A. ferox

This large tree aloe will eventually attain a height of over 3m (10ft) and a spread of over 2m (6ft), but it is attractive at any

Aloe aristata
(Guinea-fowl aloe).

size, and more modest specimens make excellent feature plants. The large and rigid blue leaves are covered in fierce prickles. It is winter-flowering. producing bright orangey-red to yellow flowers, and may survive outdoors in more favoured areas that are virtually frost-free.

A. maculata

An almost stemless and suckering aloe, perhaps better known under one of its old names, *A. saponaria*. It is widespread in the wild and there are many forms, some of which are much more hardy than others. The sparse rosettes of leaves lie close to the ground and reach 30–60cm (12–24in) in diameter. They sucker freely when bedded out and the offspring can pop up anywhere within a metre (3ft) or so of the main plant. The long, narrow leaves are toothed along the margin and traversed by bands of elongated pale dots, making them appear almost striped, and the flowers, each with a characteristic swollen base, are clustered at the tip of the flower stem. It produces reddish-orange to yellow flowers in the summer.

This species can be prone to rotting if water collects on the leaves during winter.

A. striatula

Some friends of mine who grow their succulent collection outdoors assure me that this is the most hardy of all the aloes. It has fairly slender stems and grows into a sprawling bush up to 2m (6ft) tall with rosettes about 50cm (20in) in diameter. The narrow, recurved, slightly shiny, dark green leaves distinguish it from the other 'climbing' aloes. There are a number of different forms, some more floriferous than others. Flowers are produced in the summer and are pale orangey-red to yellow in colour. It benefits from a regular prune to remove the oldest and longest stems and to keep it reasonably compact.

These plants are probably most suitable for outdoor bedding as their size and growth habit make them unstable in pots.

This species should not be confused with *A. striata*, which is almost stemless and has broad pale green leaves with paler stripes.

APTENIA

A small group of similar creeping mesembryanthemums.

Aptenia cordifolia

This fast-growing mesembryanthemum makes good ground cover and is often used abroad in dry desert areas to stabilize sandy soils. It has small fleshy, broad, pointed leaves and very small bright red flowers. It requires quite damp conditions to grow at its optimum rate.

Aptenia cordifolia.

The pretty variegated form is a little more compact and has leaves that are more yellow than green. It is ideal for a tub or urn where it can trail down over the edge of the container.

It is easy to propagate from cuttings in slightly damp compost. Rather than trying to lift the plant for overwintering indoors, it is probably best to take cuttings in autumn.

BEAUCARNEA

A little-known genus of Mexican and Central American plants, now included in the family Nolinaceae, along with *Nolina*, *Dasylirion* and *Calibanus*. All have similarities with *Yucca* but are now considered as a separate group.

Beaucarneas are borderline succulents. Although the stems of many are initially globular, on older plants they elongate, tapering towards the tip, which bears a rosette of persistent grass-like leaves. The spikes of often scented flowers are usually unisexual.

B. *recurvata* (ponytail palm)

A large plant up to 10m (30ft) tall, the tapering and branching stem growing from a thick swollen base, more than 1m (3ft) across, and capped with a dense head of grass-like leaves, which may reach 1.8m (6ft) long. The leaves persist for a long time before yellowing and eventually dropping.

Although large plants are seldom seen in cultivation in Britain, small ponytail palms are grown extensively as pot plants. They are almost globular with a head of grass-like leaves and it is many years before they swell sufficiently to start to produce adult stems. Large plants can be seen in some gardens in the south of France, but they are vulnerable to frost and snow, which will kill the tops.

Any size plant of this species is at least unusual and the larger they grow the more impressive they become. All make superb feature plants to use in any landscape, whether in pots or planted out.

B. *stricta*

Similar to *B. recurvata* except that the stems are corkier and the leaves are much shorter and stiffer. It is seldom seen in cultivation but also makes an impressive plant.

BESCHORNERIA

Semi-succulent plants now included in the agave family, species in this genus produce large rosettes of soft linear leaves and tall flower spikes up to 2m (6ft) tall. They are half-hardy in southern England if given a little protection in winter.

B. yuccoides

This is the only species usually seen in cultivation, except in specialist collections. Its tall slender and erect leaves, to 60cm (24in) long, are glaucous and light grey-green. The tall inflorescence, which is occasionally produced in Britain, is up to about 2m (6ft) tall with pendent tubular flowers in shades of red and green to yellow (see photo p.2).

BILLBERGIA

There are many species and hybrids in this genus of semi-succulent members of the pineapple family. They are fairly robust and many will tolerate low temperatures if dry. Most plants clump freely with leaves that are rigid and curlved, forming a cylinder for most of their length, their tips curving outwards. The terminal flowers are produced on mature rosettes.

Billbergia nutans.

B. *nutans* (angel tears)

Probably the most robust of the species, this may well survive outdoors in winter if given just a little protection and a well-drained compost. Its common name relates to the inflorescence of pendent tubular, green and yellow flowers, edged in blue, which are regularly produced in spring.

The leaves, rather like coarse grass, form into slender mid-green cylinders up to about 50cm (20in) tall. Plants offset profusely, soon making dense clumps.

CARPOBROTUS

This member of the mesembryanthemum family is widespread in the wild, often growing along seashores and stabilizing sand dunes; plants can be seen along the coast in the West Country where they form large colonies. Plants are often large and carpeting, and not really suitable for pot culture.

Carpobrotus edulis is also known as the Hottentot fig.

C. *edulis*

This species is the one usually cultivated. It makes large mats of rosettes of short, thick, chunky triangular leaves and, in favourable conditions, can cover quite large areas. The yellow or purple flowers require large amounts of sunshine to develop and only open in sunshine.

CARRUANTHUS

This member of the mesembryanthemum family is small, making clumps up to 60cm (24in) in diameter. The two species are very similar.

C. peersii

The short chunky keeled leaves of this rosette-forming species have a few teeth along their upper margins. It flowers quite prolifically during the summer months producing small yellow daisy-like flowers. Plants clump quite freely and will eventually make large specimens. Although it is fairly tolerant of low temperatures, it should be protected from frosts. An ideal subject for a shallow bowl or for a mixed container.

CEREUS

These tall and majestic column cacti are natives of eastern South America and the Caribbean. Originally most tall cacti were placed in this genus but many have now been split into separate genera, leaving just over 30 species here. Some are quite tropical in origin, but others come from higher and cooler habitats. The tropical species can be quite temperamental and are not suitable for outdoor planting, as they require high temperatures.

C. hildemanianus (syn. C. peruvianus)

Probably the most robust member of the genus, this species grows to 10m (30ft) in height, branching to make large tree-like plants. The stems are deeply ribbed and have large spiny cushions (areoles) from which the spines arise. They usually commence flowering when about 1.5m (5ft) tall, producing funnel-shaped, white to pale pink flowers that open at night during summer.

It is easy to grow and will quite rapidly make a good, sized plant. Give it plenty of room to grow; larger plants require substantial pots, both for stability (protect them from strong winds) and to allow room for growth.

Although tolerant of low temperatures, they need to be protected from frost in winter. If they are used for summer bedding, grow them in clay pots, which can be plunged *in situ* and lifted easily in autumn.

Cleistocatctus straussii.

CLEISTOCACTUS

Most species of this cactus genus have slender stems and long, narrow tubular flowers. The stems can be rather brittle and larger plants may require staking. In the wild, humming birds pollinate the flowers, which contain a rich supply of nectar.

C. strausii (silver torch)

A tall species up to 4m (12ft) high and branching at or near the base. The cylindrical stems, 10cm (4in) or more in diameter, are densely covered in short, hair-like spines that mask the stronger straight ones, giving the appearance of a silvery white column. Tubular red flowers, to 9cm (3½in) long, are produced in profusion in late spring on plants 60cm (24in) or more high.

This is a fairly cold-tolerant plant and may survive outdoors in a sheltered and dry position. Use a good-sized pot to allow room for growth – when under potted for any length of time the main stem tends to go blind and offsets freely from the base, making a cluster of short stems. Taller plants can be quite brittle and require staking.

A beautiful and easy plant to grow and flower, the silver torch will greatly enhance any collection of succulent plants.

COTYLEDON

A genus of mostly small bushy leafy succulents, all of which produce pendent bell-shaped flowers in the summer. Most are easy to grow and although some will tolerate low winter temperatures, they should be protected from freezing, as at best they will shed all their leaves.

C. orbiculata

There are many forms of this plant, some of which are named but many are not. Leaves vary from narrow, linear and grey to large and almost spherical, sometimes with a crinkled edge. The leaves are mostly covered with a white powder (farina), which is easily removed by touching or spraying with water.

The usual form, which is reputed to have medicinal benefits for some foot complaints, has almost round, white powdery leaves, up to 5cm (2in) across. It is small and bushy but can become untidy so regular pruning is essential to maintain an attractive plant.

Right: Cotyledon orbiculata *has orangey-red bell-shaped flowers.*

C. undulata

This has slightly larger and thicker leaves than *C. orbiculata*, the upper edge is straighter and undulating. When grown outdoors, its leaves take on a deep purple hue under the powdery white coating. The flowers are quite large in relation to the plant and are orange-red, which is very attractive in multiple plantings. Protect from frosts.

C. woodii

This bushy species grows to about 15cm (6in) tall and has small leaves that are initially green, later becoming glaucous blue-green. Although an unpretentious plant, it has relatively large brilliant red tubular flowers in spring. Larger specimens make attractive features. Protect from frosts.

CRASSULA

This is a large genus of plants in a family of the same name. The smallest species are perhaps under 2.5cm (1in) while the largest will grow to about 6m (20ft). Crassulas are leaf succulents, their leaves swollen to different degrees and in many different shapes and colours. They mostly have clusters of small white, pink or red flowers in autumn and winter. Some make attractive pot plants for patio or terrace, others are more rapid growing and can be used for summer bedding.

Most species will not tolerate frost at all. If frozen the plants rot as soon as they thaw out.

An old plant of Crassula arborescens.

C. arborescens

A large bush, up to 3m (10ft) tall, with almost round, thick bluish leaves, about 6cm (2½in) in diameter and edged in red. The plants make a thick swollen main trunk, which supports the lateral branches and heavy leaves.

Each stem of a well-grown plant will have a head of leaves so heavy that it pulls the stem downwards and may even snap it off. Prune occasionally, shortening long stems back to a side branch, to reduce weight and encourage the plants to stay more compact and grow taller. Larger plants bear pink flowers in spring.

These make attractive specimen plants and are best displayed in suitable pots or containers. Cuttings are easy to root during the summer in a gritty compost.

C. falcata (propeller plant)

The chunky, blue-grey scimitar-like leaves of this plant are arranged in a gentle spiral around its stem, becoming prostrate on the ground, and give it its common name. Dense clusters of bright red flowers appear from the tips of mature stems in late summer. They are deeply perfumed with a unique sweet smell.

Plants become untidy with time and new ones should be started from cuttings each year to provide a succession. Attractive when used as part of a summer-bedding scheme.

Crassula multicava rapidly makes large mats of plants.

C. multicava

This rapid-growing groundcover plant has thin fleshy almost round leaves. It prefers a slightly damp position and will soon make an attractive bush up to about 30cm (12in) tall. Spidery pink flowers are produced in winter to spring. After flowering the flowerheads produce little plantlets, which will soon drop and enlarge the colony.

Although extremely robust and tolerant of lower temperatures, this species is unlikely to survive more than the lightest of frosts.

C. ovata (money plant, jade plant)

This tall, tree-like species eventually grows to about 6m (20ft) tall with a thick and swollen trunk. The bright green and shiny leaves are often edged in red when grown in full sun, and flowers are arranged in small white clusters.

Crassula ovata.

It requires plenty of sunshine, food and water in summer to grow and flower well in autumn to winter, and needs a generous container, which it will soon outgrow. It makes a very attractive feature specimen outdoors in summer, but must be indoors in winter as it will be killed by frost.

Under good conditions these fast-growing plants require pruning from time to time to keep a good shape. Normally, pruned branches will offset just below the cut. Prune in spring or early summer as flower buds are initiated in midsummer. These plants grow easily from leaves or cuttings planted in a gritty compost.

Because they are robust, plants are often neglected and although they survive under poor light, where most other plants would die, they develop long, slender dejected branches and small lacklustre leaves. To rejuvenate such plants, prune them heavily in spring, leaving a good sturdy branch structure, and then repot into fresh compost. Within 2–3 months they will begin to be beautiful again.

C. sarmentosa

This fast-growing trailing species is usually seen as the variegated form with small bright green and yellow leaves that blush with red in sunshine. It is useful as a groundcover plant or for hanging baskets or other situations where it can trail.

It requires moderate amounts of water in summer and will grow quite quickly. Prune it frequently, shortening the longest stems, to keep it compact.

Cuttings root easily: it is probably better to root cuttings in late summer and overwinter these, starting with new plants each year.

DASYLIRION

A group of xerophytic shrubs, now included in the *Noline* family. They have solitary stems, densely covered in a crown of leaves, only with great age making a trunk.

D. longissimum

Unlike the more common species of this genus (*D. wheeleri*), this has dense, very long, tapering and quill-like, square slender leaves, up to 2m (6ft) long and very sharply tipped. Because of its spread it is only suitable for large plantings. It very slowly makes a thick tree-like stem, eventually growing to 2m (6ft).

It will tolerate light frosts but needs very well-drained compost.

Dasylirion wheeleri.

D. wheeleri

Perhaps the most common species in cultivation, as most are very poorly represented, this has a head of bluish–green, initially erect, slender, toothed leaves. Each leaf ends in a cluster of fibres, which look rather like a small brush.

Moderately hardy and will tolerate the occasional light frosts.

DELOSPERMA

A large group of small shrubby to prostrate members of the mesembryanthemum family. Most are easy to grow and can be readily propagated from midsummer cuttings, which may be the best way to keep plants over the winter, leaving the old plants *in situ*. Like many of the shrubby mesembryanthemums, they are perennial, but as they age, they become very woody and seem less able to assimilate food and water and so do not live very long. As only a few are in cultivation, winter hardiness has not been fully tested. They are best treated as summer-bedding plants, with any winter survivors being seen as a bonus. It is possible that as yet uncultivated species from the more mountainous areas of South Africa may have potential as bedding plants.

D. cooperi

This low shrubby species with bright pink flowers seems able to survive light frosts given a well-drained soil. Grow in a bright and sunny spot, pruning in late spring to remove any dead stems.

Delosperma cooperi.

D. nubigenum

A short trailing species with small, bright yellow flowers. Probably the most robust species so far tried, this is often sold with alpines or rock plants as being totally hardy; from experience, although it is capable of surviving light frosts, it is unlikely to survive severe weather and a wet soil. Because of its spreading habit, it makes an ideal plant to grow where it can trail over a wall or rocks, or in tubs, so that it can hang down.

DOROTHEANTHUS

A small group of annual mesembryanthemums, well known to gardeners as ice plants or Livingstone daisies.

D. bellidiformis (ice plant, Livingstone daisy)

This charming annual has fleshy, crystalline leaves which spread flat on the ground. It will grow almost anywhere but requires damp conditions to grow to its optimum size, and full sun to produce its abundant brilliant colourful summer flowers. The flowers only open in sunshine.

An ideal plant for summer bedding or tubs. Mass plantings give a riot of colour during the hot summer days, and once established will survive periods of summer drought with ease.

Dorotheanthus bellidiformis.

DROSANTHEMUM

Another group of small groundcover to shrubby plants from the mesembryanthemum family. Most have raised, glassy warts (papillae) on the leaves that make them shine in the sun, as though they have just been sprayed with water. It is an extremely widespread genus in the wild but comparatively uncommon in cultivation.

Reasonably robust, these plants are well adapted to dry conditions but are unlikely to tolerate more than light frosts. Seed is sometimes available for different species and certainly worth trying.

D. bicolor

One of the larger bushy species, up to about 50cm (20in) tall, with golden flowers shaded to reddish purple.

Drosanthemum
hispidum.

D. hispidum

A short bush up to 30cm (12in) tall but spreading to form a carpet. Small dense leaves and stems make this a charming plant, even without its brilliant purple flowers. Ideal for an area where it can be allowed to cascade.

ECHEVERIA

A large group of rosette-forming succulents, mostly almost stemless, but some making short bushes. These plants will hybridize with other related and similar genera, producing a wide range of interesting and colourful offspring. Most are quite prone to rotting if cool and damp, particularly if water collects on the leaves. A few species are relatively hardy and some are used by seaside parks departments for formal bedding and flower clocks. These are, however, unlikely to withstand more than the occasional light frost.

E. agavoides

One of the larger rosette-forming species with short, broad and pointed triangular leaves of light olive-green, often tinged with bright red around the tips. At lower temperatures, keep it dry as moisture on the leaves can easily cause rot.

These plants offset quite freely, forming large and attractive clumps, which make them ideal for low feature plants.

Echeveria agavoides × linsayana.

E. elegans

Small bluish-leaved, stemless rosettes that colour pinkish in good light. They offset quite freely and seem able to withstand short periods of light frost.

With E. glauca, this is the best species for outdoor culture in sheltered and well-drained spots.

E. glauca

The stemless rosettes of this species are cup-like and composed of broad but thin bluish leaves. They clump up easily and are much favoured by parks departments for bedding.

Together with E. elegans, probably the most hardy species and seems a little better adapted to damper conditions. Ideal for summer bedding or to make a feature plant in a broad and shallow container. (See photo, p.11).

E. nodulosa

A small bushy species with stems to about 30cm (12in) tall, bearing well-spaced, small, narrow, deep green leaves, marked with deep purple blotches or stripes and a terminal rosette. Prune from time to time to prevent it from becoming untidy; remove the longest stems, encouraging a well-shaped bush to develop. The cuttings will root quite easily if pushed into some gritty compost and kept just damp.

This species, along with a number of other echeverias, can be propagated from the leaves. Gently remove the leaves by pushing them off in a sideways direction at their union with the stem. If they come away cleanly, dry for 2–3 days and then push them into some gritty compost, just deep enough so that they will stand up. After about six weeks new plantlets should appear around the base of the leaf. Allow these to grow on until they are large enough to handle, and then pot up individually.

ECHINOCEREUS

A cactus genus often cited as being hardy. Some of the species do seem to be able to stand periods of dry cold, although in my experience this often causes the skin of the plant to become badly marked. Although a number of species come from areas that have severe frosts, most of these habitats are also very dry with a low humidity; many of these species are difficult to grow in cultivation, even in a heated greenhouse, due to high humidity.

Echinocereus cinerascens.

E. cinnerascens

A large, mounding plant, offsetting freely, with light green stems and long white spines. Larger plants flower freely in spring bearing beautiful large pink flowers with white centres. Ideal for a broad and shallow container.

Although it is a fairly robust species, it is prone to rotting in winter if kept cold and damp.

E. pentalophus

Similar to the *E. cinnerascens* except that the stems are much more slender and trailing and it is more likely to flower as a small plant. (See photo p.24).

ECHINOPSIS

Many years ago this was a smallish genera of globular plants with mostly long-tubed trumpet-shaped flowers produced at night. More recently other very similar genera have been amalgamated here. The major genus now included is *Trichocereus*, which contains tall, column-forming plants also with a long tubular flower. Although it has been suggested that other genera should be added – for example, *Lobivia*, which is usually day flowering with a shorter flower tube – and I am sure these are very closely related, here I will just include the original *Echinopsis* species and *Trichocereus*.

E. eyriesii

This old echinopsis is well-known and widely distributed in cultivation. It is an extremely robust species and will eventually develop into a short thick column up to about 30cm (12in) tall, offsetting freely to make large clumps. The plant is characterized by its shallow ribs, short black spines and white to pale pink flowers.

Like *E. oxygona* it is a very rugged plant and tolerant of all kinds of neglect and mistreatment. These are the great survivors of the cactus family.

An old plant of Echinopsis oxygona, one of the great survivors of the cactus world.

Well-cultivated specimens make beautiful large clumps and flower freely during the summer. Flowers are produced at night and most *Echinopsis* seem to bloom at the same times of the year, perhaps influenced by the phases of the moon.

E. oxygona

Like *E. eyriesii*, this is a very common species in cultivation, due to its robustness. It is a shorter plant, offsetting even more freely to make large clumps, with deeper ribs and longer, usually brown spines. The pale pink to lavender flowers are produced at night during summer.

Both the above species have been crossed with many others of this group, including *Lobivia*, to produce some beautiful colourful hybrids.

These are often intermediate between the parents giving rise to a large variety of forms, shapes and flower colours. Most are extremely robust.

E. pachanoi

This tall trichocereus is almost spineless and normally has a bluish stem. There are many other very similar plants, with or without spines, which are very closely related and perhaps are just different forms of this species. When they are about 1.5m (5ft) tall, the plants produce large white flowers, about 20cm (8in) wide, from the top of the plant, opening at night and fading the following day.

At low temperatures in glasshouses it seems prone to fungal infections that cause black marks on the stems, but these are not so likely in the moving air outdoors. These plants are well worth trying in a permanent planting, providing the soil is very well drained and that frosts are only occasional and light, but such frosts can kill the growing tops of the stems.

EUPHORBIA

The enormous spurge family contains over 1,000 succulent species, many from Africa. Many of the succulent euphorbias of the Old World have adapted to their environment in the same way as the cacti in the New World and appear similar in shape, much to the confusion of the newer collector.

Many members of this group are of tropical origins and are not tolerant of low temperatures, rotting from the top if cold, from the bottom if wet. Some of the larger species produce traditional cactus-like shapes at a relatively small size. These make excellent feature plants when used in pots and can be put outdoors during the warmer summer months, although they will need protecting during winter.

E. candelabrum

This species is very widespread in the wild and occurs from South Africa north to Saudi Arabia. Everywhere it grows, it is given a different botanical name but all these plants are basically similar. They are tall column-forming plants, branching to make large candelabra-like shapes. Depending on the origins of the

Euphorbia candelabrum *with* Furcraea selloana *var.* marginata.

plant, some are more hardy than others: those originating from South Africa are probably the most robust.

These plants are ideal for creating a cactus-like effect but will not tolerate low temperatures or wet conditions. Grow in substantial heavy pots to resist toppling in high winds.

E. resinifera

Probably one of the more robust species, able to tolerate occasional light frosts providing it is dry. The short, thick clumping stems make fine mounds. One of the few succulent species worth trying outdoors in a permanent planting in favourable areas. (see photo p.87).

FAUCARIA

These small and clumping mesembryanthemums have thick chunky leaves with wispy teeth along the edge and narrowing towards the tip. They all have golden daisy-like flowers in autumn. Despite their thick succulent leaves these plants seem surprisingly hardy and will tolerate the occasional light frost providing they are in a very free-draining compost.

They will clump freely to make plants up to about 20cm (8in) diameter and are ideal for a multiple planting or as specimens in short pots or pans. Although they may tolerate the cold, they will rot if in wet compost for any length of time. Most plants are fairly similar.

F. felina (tiger's jaw)

There are many forms of this species, all with thick, keeled leaves, tapering and with a few teeth along the edge towards the tip. The common name derives from the spreading leaves looking a little like an open mouth with teeth. Brilliant golden yellow flowers are produced in autumn and last for many days, opening fully in sunshine.

F. tuberculosa

Similar F. felina, this has slightly larger leaves with a larger number of teeth and the upper surface covered in raised white warts. It has similar cultivation requirements and makes an attractive specimen plant in a shallow pan.

Faucaria
tuberculosa.

FEROCACTUS (barrel cactus)

Many of these species grow quite large in time, some reaching 3m (10ft) tall in the wild. Although most are susceptible to low temperatures, they make outstanding feature plants in tubs or pots. Most have fierce and colourful spines, straight or hooked, and are not particularly slow-growing. Give plants a rich compost and plenty of room to grow. Add plenty of grit to the compost to make sure that is also free-draining.

During winter provide a minimum temperature of 5°C (41°F), otherwise they are prone to either rotting or at least marking badly. If a greenhouse or conservatory is not available, they make excellent indoor decorations for winter and are sure to become a talking point with friends and visitors.

F. herrerae (fish hook cactus)

This barrel cactus has long and dark, hooked spines and deep ribs. It will grow to 2m (6ft) tall and 50cm (20in) in diameter. Some forms are reputed to be among the hardiest in the genus and able to tolerate short periods of frost.

Like all members of the genus, it makes an ideal feature plant, providing that it can be placed where it will not attack admirers.

GASTERIA

An extremely variable group of plants with thick, chunky succulent leaves. When small, many species have their leaves arranged in only one plane, so looking like a fan. Some will form rosettes when mature. The strange shape of the flowers – tubular but swollen like a balloon or stomach in the middle – gives the genus its name. Tall stems produce these pendent flowers, which are mostly orangey red to yellow and green. In the wild the plants tend to grow among grasses and it seems that everywhere they appear, they are slightly different, giving rise to many forms of the same species. A major revision of the genus has recently been completed. Based on flower shape, it has resulted in a great reduction in the number of species.

The plants are easy to propagate by dividing the clumps. Many of the larger offsets will already have made roots and can be potted immediately. This is one of the few members of the Aloe family that can be propagated from leaves. Cut or break a leaf from the plant and allow to dry for a few days. Push into a very gritty and free-draining compost and keep slightly damp. New plantlets will appear from the base of the leaf in 2–3 months and after about a year can be removed and potted individually.

G. bicolor

A very variable species now embodying many old names. The leaves are mostly long, spear-shaped and shiny green with bands of pale green to white blotches. They are arranged fan shape that slowly spirals in old plants. Plants offset freely to make dense and solid clumps.

Gasteria bicolor.

An easy plant to grow, very tolerant of most conditions, except prolonged wet compost. It will tolerate short periods of light frost but long-term exposure to sub-zero temperatures will cause it to rot.

In an outdoor planting these plants can either be dotted about to make a solid dark green feature or propagated and used to make an edge to the planting. On older plants the tall spikes of flowers that grow in spring and summer add an unusual touch of colour.

G. carinata

Similar to *G. bicolor* but with shorter, chunkier leaves that are not glossy. The leaves can be spear-shaped or short and rounded at the tips, initially arranged in a fan but some soon forming a rosette. The white dots tend to be a little more pronounced and can be raised (var. *verrucosa*), sometimes arranged in bands.

Again it is easy to grow and very robust. If dry in winter, it will survive the occasional frost.

G. croucheri

This species is distinctive because of its much paler leaf colour, often an almost olive green. The leaves are of medium length and pointed, very triangular in cross section, the upper surface often concave. The plants tend to form dense rosettes of leaves and the dotted markings are fairly indistinct.

Cultivation as for the other species.

GLOTTIPHYLLUM

The abundant, yellow daisy-like flowers of this mesmebry-anthemum genus are produced throughout most of the year, even in winter, but will only open fully in the sun. The mostly bright pale green leaves are swollen and finger-like, arranged in a dense fan shape, the branches laying flat on the ground. Their major disadvantage is that they act like a magnet to the slug and snail population. To some extent the size of the plants depends on the amount of food and water they receive; they become gross and distorted if overfed.

Most species are similar and well worth growing for their bright and colourful flowers. They are easy to grow from seed or cuttings – perhaps those planted in the garden are best treated as annuals. Specimens can be grown in short pots or pans and will probably look better if potted in a fairly poor and well-drained compost. Unless they are very dehydrated, any frost will cause the leaves to freeze and collapse as soon as they thaw out.

G. longum

Now the correct name for many of the multitude of almost indistinguishable species. Details as above.

GRAPTOPETALUM

A small group of echeveria-like plants that will readily hybridize with echeverias to produce some sprawling colourful hybrids. Many of the species and hybrids are initially compact rosettes but soon make longer trailing stems with terminal rosettes. The plants need pruning from time to time to keep them compact; cut them back to short stems and remove the individual heads with a short piece of stem attached. In spring and summer the heads can be rooted easily in gritty compost and the old plant will soon branch out again.

In most species and hybrids the leaves are very loosely attached to the stem and easily knocked off. Again these can be rooted in gritty compost and will make new plants. Because of the ease of propagation, these plants can soon be bulked up to create a colourful border in a summer succulent bed.

G. paraguayense

This robust species has short, pink to grey leaves, arranged in a tight rosette at the ends of the stems. It soon becomes trailing and is best propagated each year to make more compact plants. Several heads can be rooted into a single pot to make an instant new plant.

In favourable areas it can be grown in an outdoor bed, as it seems able to tolerate the occasional frost.

Graptopetalum
paraguayense
*planted in a hole
in a wall.*

GYMNOCALYCIUM

This genus of small cacti contains many species that are like large buttons, their height being significantly less than their diameter. Although a number of the larger species have green plant bodies (or heads), many have brown or grey bodies and flower easily when small. The name *Gymnocalycium* (naked calyx) refers to the beautiful flowerbuds, which are devoid of spines or hair and in many species look almost as if they have been carved from metal. The flowers are mostly white to pale pink although there are also red- and yellow-flowered species. Borne in succession from late spring and into summer, they only open fully in sunshine.

many of these plants are from central South America, otften from cooler and arid areas, and are fairly robust, being tolerant of the occasional frost providing their roots are dry, and would probably be suitable for planting out in favoured areas. However, their small size means that they can soon be lost in a bed, so are perhaps better grown individually in pots or several together in a pan.

Gymnocalycium bruchii.

G. baldianum

The beauty of this small-growing and normally solitary plant is the bright red flowers produced from late spring to late summer. The flowers can be all shades of red, from orangey to purple. Plant several together in a pan for the best effect.

It requires full sun and regular watering in spring and summer to grow well. During winter it should be kept dry and it can then tolerate the occasional frost.

G. bruchii

A very small species with heads seldom more than 5cm (2in) across. It offsets readily and soon makes beautiful clumps densely covered in white spines. In the spring and summer it produces numerous delicate pale pink to pink flowers. It is sometimes sold as a blue-flowered cactus (which it certainly is not) due to a colour printing error in a well-known book.

It has similar cultivation requir- ements to *G. baldianum*.

G. gibbosum

The green stems of this species eventually grow tall and make a short thick column, up to 20cm (8in) tall. Although initially solitary, as it ages it slowly offsets to make a clump. White flowers are produced in spring and summer.

The larger size of this species makes it more suitable for planting in a bed in favoured areas. Cultivate in the same way as other *Gymnocalcium* species.

HAWORTHIA

A large genus belonging to the aloe family. Most are small clumping plants with thick fleshy leaves and produce tall spikes of small, whitish flowers throughout the year. They occur in diverse shapes varying from thick, fleshy pale green rosettes, to short cylindrical plants with small pointed leaves, often with bright white markings on them. Many of the species are quite variable and have a number of different forms. They are slow-growing and compact plants, ideal for inclusion in a multiple planting or as specimens in shallow containers.

Haworthias tend to grow in the shade in the wild, under bushes or protected by rocks, and are remarkably tolerant of neglect. Most are easy to grow and, providing they are dry, will tolerate low temperatures, including the occasional short period of frost. In cultivation they can be grown in full sun or shade. Those in full sun tend to colour to a deep purplish-green or an autumnal rust red, which is very attractive. In the shade, in summer, with sufficient water the plants will swell and grow well and be at their brightest green.

This group, along with the others of the aloe family, used to belong to the lily family and, like bulbs, tend to produce an annual root system when conditions permit. It is not unusual after periods of drought for them to shed most of their roots; they then need only light watering to get them back into full growth.

Most haworthias are propagated by division. Remove a clump from its compost and gently ease away the larger offsets from the base, most normally have roots and can be potted immediately. Gently push offsets without roots into gritty compost and keep slightly damp; they should root quite quickly.

H. attenuata

This is one of the most popular species in the genus and is often wrongly captioned in books as *H. fasciata*. It is a small rosette-forming plant, freely branching to make clumps. The leaves are narrow and tapering and usually have raised white dots on them, sometimes scattered, sometimes in bands. It is an easy plant to grow but does not like waterlogged conditions. It will benefit from more frequent waterings in well-drained compost. Grown in full sun, the foliage will be a dark green or purple-green, making the white dots appear even more prominent (see photo p.15).

H. cymbiformis

The soft and short, broad paler green leaves of this plant are a contrast to those of the above species. It is easy to grow, offsetting freely to make large mounded clumps of dense heads. A very variable species with many forms, most have paler translucent lines or markings along the length of their leaves.

HEREROA

The clump-forming species of this genus, which belongs to the mesembryanthemum family, have numerous small cylindrical or slightly flattened tapering leaves. Many only grow 5–8cm (2–3in) tall and produce numerous golden flowers late in the afternoon and early evening from spring to autumn. The leaves mostly have pronounced small dark dots on their leaves, visible when inspected closely.

This is an easy genus to grow and propagate from seed, the tufted clumps and bright flowers are ideal to intersperse in a multiple planting. There are many different species from a very wide range of habitats, but most are still poorly known in cultivation, in due course some will prove to be more resistant to frost than others.

H. glenensis

A small tufted species, to about 5cm (2in) tall, with slender almost cylindrical, erect leaves of dark dull green, well covered with very small darker dots. It clumps freely and soon makes fine plants. Bright yellow flowers are produced freely and intermittently from spring to autumn.

This is an easy and non-demanding plant to grow and useful for a multiple planting. It seems able to tolerate the occasional light frost if completely dry.

HESPERALOE

A small group of plants, closely related to the yuccas and agaves rather than aloes. They are short, clump-forming plants with thickened, grass-like leaves, the edges of which often break into curled fibres. Only one species is usually seen in cultivation.

H. parviflora

This plant is easy to grow, in time making large clumps (1m or more in diameter) of narrow, spear-shaped deep green leaves, edged in white fibres that break away from the leaf and curl.

The clumps can be divided to make additional plants. This is a good species for bedding in well-drained compost as it seems quite tolerant of the occasional frost. The flower spikes, much like those of an aloe, are up to 2m (6ft) tall and bear tubular pink to red flowers during the summer months. (See photo p.7.)

KALANCHOE

A large group of mostly tropical species of the crassula family. Most are quite susceptible to low temperatures and are not really suited to outdoor culture, except as summer-bedding plants. Most are dwarf to small bushes with thickened fleshy leaves, some hairy or velvety. Some also produce new plantlets around the edge of the leaves; these soon root to make a colony.

K. beharensis

This species grows to a small tree, about 3m (10ft) tall. It has large, indented and fleshy, densely velvety leaves in shades of grey to brown, which when dried are very popular with flower arrangers. Although a woody species and fairly rigid, it is quite susceptible to temperatures below about 6°C (43°F). It makes an outstanding plant for a large tub or pot and can be placed outdoors as a feature specimen during summer, and enjoyed indoors in a bright situation during winter.

Larger plants flower during spring or summer bearing spikes of small and insignificant, brownish, bell-shaped flowers.

K. daigremontiana

Children find this species fascinating because of the new plantlets that grow around the edges of the boat-shaped leaves. As the plantlets develop, they produce roots and are very easily detached, most falling to the ground and soon forming a dense colony.

Although usually seen as small plants, when it reaches about 50cm (20in) tall, this species will flower in early spring, the terminal flower spike producing numerous small grey-violet, bell-shaped flowers. The stems are fairly brittle, so they are best cut back after flowering, allowing the plants to bush out.

This is one of the easiest species to cultivate, but it is quite susceptible to frost and not really suited for permanent outdoor planting. Overwinter some of the small plants in a frost-free environment and plant them out as summer bedding. Select a couple of good specimens in autumn and pot them up as house plants for winter.

Kalanchoe tomentosa.

K. tomentosa

This attractive species grows to a bush about 50cm (20in) tall. It has long, oval leaves densely covered in short hairs, giving the appearance of velvet. The leaves are tipped with blotches of light to reddish-brown or almost black. Each seed-grown plant seems to have its own unique colouring.

Although not resistant to low temperatures, this

species makes an interesting and decorative feature plant, ideal for pot culture outdoors in summer and an interesting indoor pot plant in winter.

LAMPRANTHUS

A large genus of shrubby mesembryanthemums, up to about 60cm (24in) tall from coasts of South Africa, in mostly winter rainfall regions. This very popular group has been used extensively as permanent plantings in gardens in warm areas, such as the Mediterranean and the Channel Islands. Although only a few species are in cultivation, there are many hybrids and selected cultivars with a wide variety of bright and showy flowers in shades of white, pink, and yellow through to the brightest red. Most plants are bushy with almost cylindrical, long green to bluish leaves, which create a very Mediterranean look, even when the plant is not in flower.

Grow in full sun, as the flowers will not open fully in the shade: several plants together in a large tub make an attractive feature on a patio. Although not completely hardy, many will tolerate occasional frosts. When more of the species are cultivated, some will no doubt prove to make better garden plants than others.

As the plants age, their stems become hardened and woody, and each year they need to be pruned in the spring to remove dead growth and again after flowering to tidy the plant. It is important to remove old and dead branches to allow a good air flow through. Many species are better restarted from cuttings every few years; old and woody plants seem to lose their vitality. Take cuttings in early summer, dry them for a couple of days and then pot them into some gritty and well-drained compost. If kept slightly damp, the cuttings should root in about 4–6 weeks and can be potted individually.

Lampranthus spectabilis.

L. haworthii

This species makes a superb plant either for a large tub or outdoor planting in favoured areas and is well worth including in any collection. When in bloom in spring it is one of the most spectacular of the genus, the bright pink, 5cm (2in) flowers completely covering the plant for several weeks. If conditions are good a few flowers may also be produced during late summer and autumn.

As this makes a large bush in time (up to 3m diamater, 1m tall), prune it back after flowering (older plants can be pruned hard) to keep it compact. During autumn it will grow vigorously and begin to develop the following year's flowers.

L. spectabilis

This bushy species grows to about 30cm (12in) tall and spreads to make clumps. Brilliant purple flowers are produced during summer.

Able to tolerate the occasional light frost.

LEWISIA

Although this genus is native of the mountainous areas of western North America, most species are temperamental and really only suited to the more specialist alpine grower. The exceptions are the various hybrids of *L. cotyledon*, which are now usually available from most garden centres.

L. cotyledon

Lewisia cotyledon.

These hybrids are available in a tremendous variety of flower colour from white, yellow through to oranges and reds and purple. The plants are mainly spring-flowering with occasional flowers produced later in the year. As they tend to be semi-dormant in the summer and can easily rot if waterlogged, they need free-draining compost and are probably best planted on a steep bank or between rocks in a wall, where drainage is not a problem.

The short fleshy stems produce rosettes of slightly fleshy leaves of various shapes, depending on their parentage. Plant several together to make a colony, which will then self seed and maintain itself, even if some of the older plants should rot off.

They are easy to grow from seed, sown in late summer in a warm spot to achieve the best results – few will germinate in the spring. Offsets are also produced.

LOBIVIA

This cactus genus is now often included in *Echinopsis*. Natives of the higher altitudes of central South America, most lobivias are tolerant of the occasional frost providing that they are kept dry. Most are day-flowering, and many are also free-flowering, although the flowers are generally short lived. Most plants are small, often clumping to make fine mounds.

L. hertrichiana

The small heads of this densely clumping species rarely exceed 5cm (2in) in diameter, although clumps can become quite sizeable. They are bright green and produce mostly bright red flowers over a period during the summer months.

One of the easiest of this group to grow, this species is tolerant of low temperatures in a very free-draining compost. Ideal for either pot culture or bedding in favoured areas.

Lobivia backebergii *subsp.* hertrichiana.

MAMMILLARIA

This is probably the most popular and widely cultivated genus of the cactus family. Most are small globular to short cylindrical plants, many offsetting to make fine clumps. The small bright flowers are produced in rings around the crown of the plant, often in spring, but some species flower at other times of the year.

In the wild, these mostly Mexican plants come from quite diverse habitats, some quite cold, some quite tropical, most are arid, although some grow in the shade of trees. Many grow in rocky ground and no doubt this retains some warmth, which helps the plants overcome the low night air temperatures.

Frequently grown as pot plants in the glasshouse, some species seem to be able to withstand the occasional light frost without damage, providing they have a well-drained compost and are fairly dry at the roots. When grown outdoors in summer, many take on red to purple body hues and have a much closer spination than those grown in a glasshouse. They make wonderful specimens and are ideal for pots or summer bedding. Only a few species are likely to be able to survive the rigors of a British winter, even in favoured areas.

M. karwinskiana

This is a branching species – a growing point periodically divides into two parts that grow into separate heads, eventually making large, old multi-headed plants that can grow up to 2–3m in diameter. Among the straight spines are numerous softer, hair-like spines that make the plants appear quite woolly. Small pink to cream flowers are produced in rings around the crowns during spring and summer. These are followed by numerous, long, sausage-shaped, bright red seedpods.

Outdoors, the plant bodies rapidly take on a purple colour, which makes the white spination even more attractive.

This seems to be quite a robust species, able to withstand the occasional frost without detriment. Certainly worth trying in an outside bed in favoured areas.

M. magnimamma

Many of the old names for very similar plants have now been put together under this title. The plants are generally large with the main heads up to about 13cm (5in) in diameter, but most clumping in time to make large mounds up to 60cm (24in) or more across. They are fairly open with long and often angular, rigid tubercles and few spines, although some of these can be several centimetres long.

Small carmine, pink or white flowers are produced in rings around the crowns in late spring. These plants seem to benefit from summer sunshine outdoors and most take on a deep purplish body tint. Long, sausage-shaped, or shorter and more swollen, red fruit are produced in late summer and autumn, adding interest and colour.

Mammillaria magnimamma.

One of the easiest mammillarias to grow and remarkably robust, being able to tolerate the occasional light frost. It is ideal for either bedding in favoured areas or for cultivation in pots.

M. polythele

This species is cylindrical, making thick broad columns, which, with great age, become trailing stems. Plant heads tend to remain solitary, although old specimens are likely to branch occasionally from the base. As with *M. magnimamma*, numerous old species have been put together under this name and they are, therefore, quite variable. Spination is mostly short and straight and reasonably dense, but the plant body can still be seen through them.

These plants flower in spring, but often produce a second crop of flowers in late summer. Flowers are followed by small, sausage-shaped seed pods, purplish in colour but not particularly significant.

Some plants seem to be quite robust and capable of withstanding the occasional frost. Grow in well-drained compost and support old trailing stems with rocks so that they are not in contact with wet soil. Worth trying outdoors in permanent plantings in favoured areas.

NOTOCACTUS

This group of mostly globular to short cylindrical cacti now belongs in the genus *Parodia*. It is, however, much better known under its old name and in general is easier to grow than those species in the old genus *Parodia*.

Many are not tolerant of low temperatures but some are much tougher than others. Like many of the cacti, they may tolerate the occasional frost, as long as they are completely dry, which makes growing them outdoors and unprotected throughout the year almost impossible.

N. leninghausii

This distinctive species makes short columnar stems, densely covered in golden spines that almost conceal the plant body; the flattish heads are covered in pale gold hair and always point towards the sun (see photo p.21). With great age the main stem can grow to about 75cm (30in) tall. The plants offset freely and soon make fine clumps. Plants flower when about 15cm (6in) tall bearing large, papery yellow flowers, with yellow stigmas, around the crown. Larger plants produce numerous blooms at the same time, several times during the summer months.

A fairly robust species, making a superb specimen in any collection, this will tolerate the occasional frost if completely dry.

Notocactus
mammulosus.

N. mammulosus

Probably one of the most robust species in this genus, and one of the least demanding, this is a small globular plant with broad ribs and short spines. Like the majority of *Notocactus*, it has large, bright buttercup-yellow flowers with glossy petals. The majority of yellow-flowered species also have red-purple stigmas. Each flower lasts for several days, opening fully in the sunshine.

There are many forms of this species, which, if completely dry, will tolerate the occasional frost. It may survive outdoors in particularly favoured areas.

OPUNTIA (prickly pear)

The prickly pear is one of the largest and most widely spread groups of the cactus family, growing from just into Canada, south to Chile and Argentina. The species are quite diverse in form, from the small alpine groundcovering clumps of the Andes in South America to the bushy or tree-like, flat padded or cylindrical stems of Mexico and West Indies or the small ground-hugging plants of northern North America.

Because the group is so widespread, many species occur over a wide range of habitats and have evolved many different forms. This makes identification extremely difficult and has given rise to several different classification systems, with the main genus split into smaller genera or groups. As these are generally little understood and very variable, many plants in cultivation are given erroneous names or just called 'species'.

Also due to their wide geographical spread, some clones of a species may be hardy, while others are far less so. Many of the cold natural habitats are usually dry too so the plants enter the cold period in a dehydrated state. Some, like the Canadian species, are covered in snow in early winter, which protects them from the cold and also keeps them fairly dry. A recent experiment in the European Alps showed that plants buried under the snow in early winter were at an almost constant temperature of -1°C (30°F) despite the air temperatures dropping substantially below this. The plants seemed to go into hibernation until the spring, when the snow melted and bright sun warmed them again.

Although there are a number of forms or species that may survive outdoors in a garden throughout the year, most will probably need winter protection from a cloche or something similar to keep them dry. I have tried numerous 'hardy' species outdoors in an unprotected, well-drained rockery; while the plants survived, with the odd pad rotting off, they made little growth.

Most opuntias are easy to propagate from cuttings so it is well worth propagating a few extra plants and trying these outdoors. Different clones will react differently to differing conditions. As a rough guide, the small, padded and spiny 'Tephrocactus' group is likely to prove the most hardy, along with a few of the smaller and spiny flat-padded species.

Opuntia engelmannii.

O. engelmannii

This species name contains a large number of different forms, some of which certainly are not hardy. The form *cantabrigiensis* is low-growing with ovoid, flattened stem segments, clumping to make dense plants, and it seems to be particularly hardy. It is known from Cambridge Botanic Garden, where it has grown for many years, and should prove hardy as a garden plant in southern gardens, providing it is grown in a very free-draining compost and full sunshine. Flowers of 5–8cm (2–3in) appear in the summer, and are mostly yellow, but sometimes reddish.

O. humifusa

This name now embodies most of the hardy species from the eastern states of the USA. Plants are small, low-growing, spiny or almost spineless with flattened stem segments often laying flat on the ground (see photo p.20). In cultivation a free-draining gritty compost, top dressed with gravel will help to keep the pads off the wet ground. Despite its cold natural habitats, it will do better if it is protected by a cloche or similar during winter. Yellow flowers are produced in the summer.

O. phaeacantha

A flat-padded species making wide clumps up to 70cm (28in) or more tall. Some of the smaller forms, up to 30cm (12in) are reputedly fairly robust and tolerant of occasional low temperatures. A very widespread and variable form in the wild, and individual plants will vary as to their cold tolerance. It is a species worth propagating and trying in an outdoor location.

PORTULACARIA

A group of two similar species, only one of which is normally seen in cultivation.

P. afra

A shrubby to tree-like species, with succulent, small and rounded bright green leaves and reddish stems, the main trunk swelling with age. In cultivation its long branches hang in a weeping style, reminiscent of a natural bonsai, and it makes an unusual and impressive feature plant when grown well. In South Africa it is often used as a hedging plant.

This is an easy plant to grow and propagate from cuttings, providing it is not allowed to get too cold. It is not hardy and requires a minimum winter temperature of at least 5°C (41°F), but makes an excellent house plant. Give plants good-sized pots and prune occasionally to preserve their shape.

There is also a pretty variegated form with green and yellow leaves, suffused with red when grown in the sunshine. It is much slower growing.

Portulacaria afra f. variegata.

PUYA

These semi-succulent members of the pineapple family are mostly found on the upper slopes of the Andes where they tolerate extremes of weather. They are probably the most robust of the bromeliads and many of the larger species will tolerate the British weather in favoured areas. The problem is not so much the cold but the wet, dull and humid winters. Left unprotected most are likely to suffer some damage to the leaves.

The species vary from small mound-forming ground-coverers, to large trunk-forming plants. The taller species are of the most interest. In the wild most form very large colonies. They can be easily grown from seed, although they may take many years to get to flowering size. Plants and seeds are normally only available from specialist suppliers.

P. alpestris

A large species from the dry Chilean Andes with narrow toothed leaves up to 1m (3ft) long. In favoured situations and in well-drained compost, it should survive outdoors, although some damage may occur to the foliage in winter. If it can be protected from the weather but without restricting the airflow around it, it will probably do much better. Although these plants can be grown in pots for the first few years, as they become large the fiercely toothed leaves make it difficult to move them. The plants produce tall inflorescences with 5cm (2in) long, deep blue flowers, and turn purple red after flowering (see photo p.19).

Worth trying bedded out in a sheltered but sunny position in favoured climates.

P. chilensis

This is another tall species from the dry mountains of Chile. It grows to about 1m (3ft) tall and branches freely. The leaves are a little broader than those of P. alpestris but are a similar length with numerous hooked spines. The inflorescences produced are up to 1.5m (5ft) tall, with yellow to green flowers that are 8cm (3in) long.

Cultivation requirements are similar to those of P. alpestris, although this species is marginally more robust.

REBUTIA

A very variable genus of small globular cacti that produce relatively large flowers in profusion in spring. They are easy plants to grow, most being propagated from seed. Some species seem quite tolerant of low temperatures in winter, more so if kept dry. The genus has had a major revision in recent years, resulting in the 800 or so old names being reduced to 50 or so species. As always happens, there is now one name covering many visually quite different plants.

Rebutias are small with heads 2.5–5cm (1–2in) across, but often clump-forming and making dense mounds up to 20cm (8in) in diameter. When grown from seed, many will flower when perhaps only two years old and little more than pea size. The flowers are mostly 2–3cm (¾–1¼in) diameter and bright red, orange, purple or yellow. A tiny plant with 7–8 large flowers on it is quite spectacular. The blooms last for several days, opening fully in the sunshine.

For cacti, rebutias are comparatively short-lived, up to 15–20 years in general. Propagate old plants every few years from cuttings or grow new plants from seed.

R. fiebrigii

This very variable species can be globular or makes slightly taller swollen stems, which can be bright green with few spines, brown to orange or completely covered with dense, short white spines. Flowers are generally orange – from orange-red to pale orange – and up to about 2cm (¾in) across and more funnel-shaped than some species.

Tolerant of occasional light frosts in winter if kept dry, it is an easy species to grow and flower and suitable for larger multiple plantings in containers or as single specimens.

R. minuscula

This species now encompasses most of the old genus of *Rebutia*. Plants normally have one main head up to about 5–8cm (2–3in) in diameter, offsetting to make clumps with the main head predominant. The heads are short and globular, usually depressed in the crown, and the spines can be extremely variable from short and brown through to dense, long and white. The flowers are freely produced from the base of the plant in spring; they open wide, often 2.5cm (1in) or more across, and are mostly shades of red, from pale orangey-red through to deep purplish-red. Many will flower in their second season from seed.

These are easy plants to grow and tolerant of much neglect. They also seem able to tolerate low winter temperatures, even if wet, although they are much better if kept dry.

R. pygmaea

A small species making a tuberous base with short, erect, finger-like, often brownish stems. Like most of the current *Rebutia* species, these are extremely variable with mostly short but very variable spines, and flowers of many colours, from white through pale pinks and oranges, to red and violet. They will flower at 2–3 years old from seed and slowly clump up – an old multi-stemmed plant will probably be less than 10cm (4in) across.

Although they are able to tolerate low temperatures, because of their tuberous root, they really need to be dry during their winter rest.

Rebutia pygmaea.

RUSCHIA

This is the largest and most widespread genus of the mesembryanthemum family, having 400 members. Plants are creeping, bushy or shrubby and despite their wide dispersal in the wild are not well-known in cultivation. Because of their diverse habitats some will no doubt prove to be much better able to adapt to the occasional frosts of favoured areas of Britain. Their small bright flowers create a Mediterranean atmosphere in any planting.

Most are easy to propagate from seed or cuttings and will make small plants within a year. It is worth trying new species outdoors in summer and rooting some cuttings in late summer, overwintering these in a frost-free environment. The old plants can then be left *in situ* in favourable areas to test for hardiness. If need be they can be replaced from the propagations.

R. maxima

Probably the tallest growing species, this makes a bush up to about 1.5m (5ft) tall. It is pyramidal with bluish, vertically flattened, sickle-shaped leaves. Plants more than 60cm (24in) high should flower well, producing bright pink flowers in early spring.

This species makes an interesting and unusual feature plant and seems able to tolerate the occasional light frost, but if grown in pots, it is probably worth protecting during the winter.

SEDUM

This large genus of the crassula family has a very wide distribution, mostly in the northern hemisphere. Nearly all come from arid and well-drained areas, where other vegetation is limited. Some occur in dry mountainous regions and are totally hardy in Britain, while others are much closer to the equator and will not tolerate frost at all.

Sedums have leaves arranged in rosettes, although in many species the rosette is not well developed. There are many species and cultivars that are popular garden plants, often sold as alpine or rockery plants as they require a well-drained compost. A few are herbaceous and suitable for borders.

Probably the prettiest sedums are the truly succulent species, many from Mexico, which have attractive colourful foliage and shapes. Unfortunately most of these are not hardy and, therefore, not suitable for outdoor planting.

S. acre (common stonecrop)

This small (up to 10cm/4in tall) species has tiny erect branches closely covered in small leaves and produces masses of 2cm yellow flowers in early summer. Its small growth and robust habit make it ideal for planting in gravel beds, between paving stones or cracks in walls, and allowing it to form carpets in beds or borders. It is completely hardy and requires virtually no maintenance. **'Aureum'** has bright yellow leaves.

Sedum acre *'Aureum' growing in a rockery.*

S. cauticola

This very variable species has sub-erect stems up to 30cm (12in) long , soon forming a loose carpet of small round-leafed rosettes, glaucous grey with purple spotting. The plants look at their best in autumn when grown in a well-drained scree and the rosettes are topped with putple flowers.

S. erythrosticum (better known as S. alboroseum)

Very similar to *S. spectabile* but often slightly taller growing. The showy September flowers have white petals and rosy carpels which then make them easy to distinguish. Cultivation as for *S. spectabile*.

S. kamtschaticum

A very variable species of short spreading stems, usually up to about 10cm (4in) tall. The stems soon spread to make a dense carpet of rosettes of small, often dark green leaves. After the summer flowers, which are usually yellow, the rosettes of many forms will bronze or redden in the sun.

One of the less succulent species and may require watering during extended periods of drought.

S. spathulifolium

The small (2–3cm/1in) rosettes of this species are stoloniferous and soon make small hummocks with small grey-green leaves that are often flushed with red or purple when grown in full sun. It produces bright yellow heads of flowers in spring.

'Cape Blanco' has grey-white leaves and makes an outstanding small feature in any planting, with its contrasting silvery colour. 'Purpureum' has red-purple foliage.

Although these plants are completely hardy, a well-drained compost is advisable as they can rot in winter if waterlogged.

❋ S. spectabile (ice plant)

This popular herbaceous perennial from China is well-known as a garden plant. The short (45cm/18in) bushes have pale whitish green leaves and produce large, pinky-mauve flowerheads in autumn. The flowers attract butterflies, which feed on the nectar. There are several varieties with slightly different flower colours, such as 'Brilliant', 'Iceberg' and 'Stardust'.

The foliage dies down in the winter and in the spring many new shoots grow from the base of the stems. To propagate, lift in late spring and divide, even the smallest shoot makes a new plant.

Although quite hardy, avoid areas that stay very wet in winter or it is liable to rot. (See photo p.23). ❋

SEMPERVIVUM (Houseleek)

Apart from *Sedum*, this is probably the only genus of succulent plants that is almost totally hardy. There are currently about 40 different species and several hundred cultivars. They are native to the mountainous areas of Europe, growing mostly between 1,000–2,500m (3,000–8,000ft).

The species often come from quite widely separated habitats, which has an effect on their form. They are, therefore, extremely difficult to identify and often this can only be achieved by comparing unidentified plants with those from a known habitat. In the wild, the three species below sometimes overlap their habitats and many of the cultivated hybrids are crosses between them. It is almost impossible to identify hybrids with any degree of certainty if they have lost their original label.

Sempervivums need a very well-drained growing area – pot or bed – with about 50 per cent sand and grit mixed with the compost. These interesting plants prefer a shallow growing medium, which makes them ideal for growing on walls or over rocks, on tufa rock or even on slate roofs (hence the common name), where traditionally they keep away evil spirits! Most are completely temperature-hardy but a few (particularly those with hairy leaves) may rot in winter unless sheltered from the rain. However, while they might like winter protection, growing them in a glasshouse in summer will rapidly make them elongate and lose their colour – even after just a couple of days.

All have terminal flowers. The growing point in the rosette develops into the flower stems that carry mostly pinkish red to yellow flowers. After flowering the rosette will die. Most sempervivums produce numerous offsets on stolons during their life, which rapidly make colonies, replacing any that have flowered. These will in turn flower in about 2–3 years.

Sempervivum tectorum with pink flower growing on a dry stone wall.

S. *arachnoideum* (cobweb houseleek)

This attractive and easy to grow well-known species has a very wide distribution in the wild. Its common name is due to the sometimes dense covering of long hairs over the leaves. In a bright sunny position, the plants can be 1–2cm (1/2–3/4in) or less in diameter and vary from green to bright red. It is one of the very few species that can be grown successfully throughout

the year in a greenhouse, where the rosettes will usually grow larger and are also much more heavily covered in cobwebs. These plants prolifically produce offsets on long stolons and will rapidly make colonies.

S. montanum

Another very widely distributed species with rosettes 2–3cm (¾– 1¼in) or more across. The bright green rosettes often have darker tips to the leaves and eventually form large mats. An easy species to grow.

S. tectorum (common houseleek)

This larger species, 5–8cm (2–3in) across, has light to dark green leaves often with red to purple tips. It clumps up well to make attractive colonies.

An easy and attractive species to grow. There are many hybrids with similar characteristics.

STOMATIUM

A genus of small, carpeting mesembryanthemums with small and swollen, chunky leaves that have small teeth along their margins. The small mostly yellow or white flowers open in the evening and are scented in some species. A recent major revision of the genus has led to many name changes and uncertain identifications.

These seem to be fairly robust plants and at least some plants (unidentified) seem able to stand the occasional frost if kept dry.

S. patulum

This has larger leaves than many in the genus, up to 2cm (¾in) long and quite swollen, with prominent teeth. Yellowish flowers appear during summer and autumn.

TRADESCANTIA

A large group of trailing plants with one species usually accepted as succulent.

T. navicularis

A strange trailing plant with side branches making dense clusters of small boat-shaped leaves, one inside the other. Given plenty of water, this plant will grow long trailing stems clothed with deep green to reddish-brown leaves and is of more interest as a good house plant. If, on the other hand, it is grown in full sun in a poor and well-drained compost, it stays much more compact and the leaves are bright red, like rubies – this outstanding colour makes it well worth growing.

It is an simple plant to grow and almost propagates itself so it can easily be replaced each year. Allow it to creep about in the early part of the year and then keep dry through the height of summer.

Tradescantia navicularis.

TRICHODIADEMA

A very widespread genus of small bushy or shrubby mesembryanthemums, some of which have tuberous roots. It mostly occurs in pastures, growing rapidly after rain. The main characteristic is the 'diadem' – a tufted cluster of spines at the end of each leaf.

These are popular as garden plants in Mediterranean areas and are mainly robust plants, tolerant of drought and the occasional frost. Most species flower freely throughout the summer and autumn. There seem to be a number of hybrids and cultivars with different flower colours.

T. mirabile

This attractive small bush has small, dark green, sausage-shaped leaves with a blackish-brown diadem. White flowers are produced throughout summer and autumn.

Grown in a well-drained compost, and kept dry in winter, it will tolerate the occasional frost in favoured areas.

YUCCA

A widely cultivated group of woody perennials from the North American continent, stretching south to Mexico. Apart from the 40–50 species there are perhaps four times that number of synonyms or unresolved names. Many of the plants are very similar, making their identification extremely difficult, particularly as many do not take on their adult characteristics until they are quite large. Many of the house plants sold as yuccas are, in fact, cordylines.

The plants can be stemless, making large rosettes of long spear-shaped leaves, or trunk-forming, up to several metres tall, some branching, some solitary, with a terminal rosette of leaves. Different species flower at various times of the year but the larger ones are unlikely to flower until mature. The normally white, bell-shaped flowers are produced on tall spikes.

Some yuccas are from very cold natural habitats and seem quite hardy in Europe, providing they are given a free-draining compost as they are more susceptible to damp than cold. Because of their size, larger plants grow better when planted directly in the ground. Smaller and juvenile plants can be used decoratively as pot plants or feature plants during the summer.

The following yucca species are reputedly hardy in Europe. As these plants are often more susceptible to wet and high humidity than cold, grow them in a very free-draining compost: *Y. arkansana, Y. angustissima, Y. baccata, Y. baileyi, Y. elata, Y. filamentosa, Y. glauca, Y. gloriosa, Y. harrimaniae, Y. pallida, Y. recurvifolia.*

These yuccas may be hardy in favoured spots with only occasional light frosts: *Y. aloifolia, Y. carnerosana, Y. filifera, Y. flaccida, Y. rostrata, Y. schidigera, Y. schottii.*

Yucca gloriosa.

Y. elata

A large species, up to 4.5m (15ft) tall, often branching, with dense heads of long, pale green to yellowish-green leaves, up to 1m (3ft) long. The old leaves are persistent, drying and hanging like a skirt around the stems.

✱ Reputed to be completely hardy.

Y. filamentosa (Adam's needle)

A virtually stemless species, spreading by stolons and forming large clumps, of green, sometimes glaucous, flexible, erect and spreading leaves. The plants will grow to 75–100cm (30–39in) tall and flower when quite young, perhaps 2–3 years old from seed. **'Bright Edge'** and **'Variegata'** have striped leaves.

✱ Reputed to be completely hardy in a well-drained compost.

Y. gloriosa (Spanish dagger)

This is probably the widest grown of all the yuccas. It is reputedly quite hardy in Britain, providing it is grown in a well-drained situation. The mostly solitary stems can reach a height of 5m (16½ft). The leaves form a dense rosette at the tips of the stems and are stiff and erect, glaucous when young, and flexible towards their tips. **'Variegata'** has striped leaves.

Plants can often flower when about five years old, producing flower stems, 1.5–2.5m (5–8ft) tall, late in the year.

FURTHER INFORMATION

BOOKS

Principal Reference works

The Agaves of Continental North America, Howard Scott Gentry
(University of Arizona Press, 1982)

Agaves, Yuccas and Related Plants, Mary and Gary Irish
(Timber Press, 2000)

Bromeliads for Home and Garden, Werner Rauh,
(Blandford, 1979)

The Cactus Family, Edward F. Anderson and Roger Brown,
(Timber Press, 2001)

CITES Cactaceae checklist, David Hunt (Royal Botanic
Gardens, Kew. 1999)

Illustrated handbook of succulent plants – In several volumes,
various authors – some sections still to be published.
(Springer-Verlag, New York, 2001 onwards)

Lexicon of Succulent Plants, Herman Jacobsen,
(Blandford, 1974)

Sedum, cultivated stonecrops, Ray Stephenson
(Timber Press, 1994)

Sempervivum & Jovibarba Handbook, P. J. Mitchell
(Sempervivum   Society, 1973)

Plus innumerable books on cacti and succulents., gardening
encyclopaedias and general gardening books.

*A bed of
Euphorbia
resinifera.*

INTERNET RESOURCES

Probably the best resource is the **Cactus Mall**, which has links to all the major sites worldwide for Cactus and Succulent plants. It includes Nurseries, Societies, Seed sellers, Book sellers, Gardens etc. It is also kept up to date with the latest links available from just one source - **www.cactus-mall.com**
also **NCCPG www.nccpg.com**
Discussion group **www.ukoasis.co.uk**
Encyclopedia **www.desert-tropicals.com**

For seeds

Doug and Viv Rowland (UK) at **www.cactus-mall.com/ rowland/index.html**
Mesa Garden (USA) at **www.mesagarden.com**
Kohres (Germany) at **www.koehres-kaktus.de/index1.htm**

For Agaves (UK)

The Agave Pages (Jan Kolendo)
www.users.globalnet.co.uk/~jankol
Oasis Designs (Paul Spracklin) **www.oasisdesigns.co.uk**
Agavaceae www.agavaceae.com (the family in great detail)
www.users.globalnet.co.uk/~exotic/oasis1.htm

For Agaves and Yuccas (USA)

Mesa Garden at **www.mesagarden.com**
Yucca Do Nursery at **www.yuccado.com/plants**
American Desert Plants at **www.desertplants.com**
Starr Nursery (specialises in agavaceae) at **www.starr-nursery.com**

CACTUS GARDENS

Holly Gate Cactus Garden (Terry Hewitt), Ashington, West Sussex. **www.hollygatecactus.co.uk**
Wide range of Cacti and Succulents landscaped in over 930m^2 (10,000sq ft) of Glasshouses.

COLLECTIONS TO VISIT

The gardens below have a range of hardy and half hardy exotics:

Cornwall

Tresco Abbey Gardens, Tresco, Isles of Scilly
Tel: 01720 424105; www.tresco.co.uk
By far the best, though not many cacti, they have the most fantastic range of succulents, many mature. Agaves and aloes like you wouldn't believe.
St Michaels Mount, Marazion
www.cornishlight.co.uk/st-michaels-mount.htm
The cliffs and rock faces surrounding the castle on here are dripping with great succulent plantings, though again not many cacti.
The grounds of the Minack Theatre, Porthcurno
Tel: 01736 810181; www.minack.com
These are being landscaped by Neil Milligan and are pretty impressive.
Lamorran House Gardens, Upper Castle Road, St Mawes
TR2 5BZ, Tel: 01326 270800; www.gardensincornwall.co.uk/lamorran/gardeninfo.htm
A mediterranean style garden with sucuclents and palms.
Queen Mary Gardens, Falmouth
A municiple garden, right on the seafront, has good succulent plantings.

Dorset

Abbotsbury Subtropical Gardens, Bullers Way, Abbotsbury, Dorset, DT3 4LA Tel: 01305 871387/871153
www.abbotsbury-tourism.co.uk/gardens.html

Essex:

Private gardenin South Benfleet, open by appointment only (Paul Spracklin, Tel: 01268 757666);
www.oasisdesigns.co.uk/my garden.htm.
Experimenting with the widest range of cacti and succulents to be found growing outside in the UK

London

The Royal Botanic Garden Kew, Surrey
Tel: 020 8332 5655; **www.rbgkew.org.uk**
Wide range of indoor and outdoor plants.

Scotland

The Royal Botanic Gardens, Edinburgh and Logan
A wide range of indoor and outdoor plants.
www.rbge.org.uk
Royal Botanic Garden Edinburgh, 20a Inverleith Row,
Edinburgh, EH3 5LR Tel: 0131 552 7171
Logan Botanic Garden, Port Logan, Stranraer, Wigtownshire,
DG9 9ND Tel: 01776 860231

Europe

Les Cedres – private succulent collection on Cap Ferrat,
Cote d'Azur, France
Jardin Botanique Nice, Cote d'Azur, France –
French National Collection of Agaves
Jardin Exotique, Monaco
Giardino Esotico Pallanca, Bordighera, Italy
Hanbury Gardens, La Mortola (near Ventimiglia), Italy
Botanical Gardens, Munich
Palmengarten, Frankfurt
Stadt Sukkulentensammlung, Zurich
Pinya de Rosa, near Blanes, Spain
Marimutra, Blanes, Spain

Plus many other Cactus and Succulent gardens in the more
Mediterranean areas.

NURSERIES

As well as those listed here there are many other links on the
Cactus Mall (**www.catctus-mall.com**).

Cacti and Succulent plants

Holly Gate Cactus Nursery, Ashington, West Sussex
Tel: 01903 892930; **www.hollygatecactus.co.uk**
Wide range of cactus and succulent plants.

Glenhirst Cactus Nursery, Station Road, Swineshead, Boston, Lincs Tel: 01205 820314; **www.glenhirstcactiandpalms.co.uk**
Range of plants, they have an interest in cold hardy succulents.
Henri Kuentz (France) for Agaves
Tel: +33 494 514 866; **www.kuentz.com**
Jean Audissou (France) for Agaves
Tel: +33 546 841 348; **perso.wanadoo.fr/jean-andre. audissou/index.htm**

Hardy and semi-hardy exotics

Architectural Plants, ooks Farm, Nuthurst, Horsham, West Sussex Tel: 01403 891772; **www.architecturalplants.com**
Many larger specimen plants.
Big Plant Nursery, Hole Street, Ashington, West Sussex.
Tel: 01903 891466; **www.bigplantsdirect.co.uk**
Good range of sizes and species.
Hardy Exotics Nursery, Gilly Lane, Whitecross, Penzance, Cornwall   Tel: 01736 740660; **www.hardyexotics.co.uk**
Good range.
Trevena Cross Nurseries, Breage, Helston, Cornwall
Tel: 01736 763880; **www.trevenacross.co.uk**
A wide range of plants.
Tresidder Farm Plants, Neil Milligan, Tressider Farm, St Buryan, Penzance, Cornwall
Good range of plants.

INDEX

Page numbers in **bold** refer
to illustrations

Index compiled by Indexing Specialists
(UK) Ltd.

The Publisher would like to thank the following people for their kind permission to reproduce their photographs:

Jacket image: Steven Wooster
Garden Picture Library: p. 11(Marie O'Hara), 40 (Georgia Glynn-Smith), 42 (JS Sira), 45 (John Ferro Sims), 46 (Chris Burrows), 48 and 63 (Jerry Pavia), 78 (Didery Willery), 81 (Sunniva Harte), 85 (Robert Estall)
Garden World Images/Keith Laban: p.41, 54, 67,69, 73, 76, 82.
All other photographs: Garden World Images